Relationship Playbook

Activities to build trust, strength, stability, and fun to your significant relationships

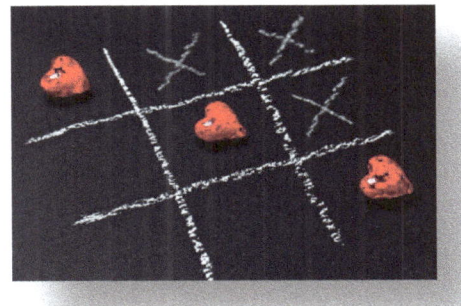

Cher Holton, Ph.D.
Bil Holton, Ph.D.

Prosperity Publishing House

I0389255

Copyright ©2023 Cher Holton, Bil Holton
All rights reserved.

Reproduction or translation of any part of this work beyond that permitted by Section 107 or 108 of the 1976 United States Copyright Act without the permission of the copyright owner is unlawful. Requests for permission or further information should be addressed to the authors, c/o Prosperity Publishing House, 1405 Autumn Ridge Drive, Durham, NC 27712.

This publication is designed to provide accurate and authoritative information in regard to the subject matter covered. It is sold with the understanding that the authors and publisher are not engaged in rendering legal, accounting, or professional therapeutic services. If legal advice or other expert assistance is required, the services of a competent professional person should be sought. Neither the authors nor publishers are liable or responsible to any person or entity with respect to any loss or damage caused or alleged to be caused directly or indirectly by this book. *From a Declaration of Principles jointly adopted by a Committee of the American Bar Association and a Committee of Publishers.*

Ordering Information:
Prosperity Publishing House
    1405 Autumn Ridge Drive, Durham, NC 27712 USA
    https://HoltonProductMall.com

Library of Congress Cataloging-in-Publication Data

Holton, Cher and Bil Holton
Relationship Playbook / Cher Holton and Bil Holton

    ISBN 978-1-946291-21-9 (print)
    ISBN 978-1-946291-22-6 (eBook, PDF)
    ISBN 978-1-946291-23-3 (Kindle)

Library of Congress Control Number: 2022950821
Printed in the United States of America
10 9 8 7 6 5 4 3 2 1

Dedicated to every couple brave enough to claim their love for one another, and willing to put in the work (and play) to keep their relationship strong.

Table of Contents

Cuddle Up for Our Pre-Read Huddle 1
    How to Use This Book 5
    What's In This Book 5
    Choosing What to Do! 7
    Final Thoughts Before You Begin! 9

Relationship Hors d'Oeuvres:
    Thoughts to Ponder…Together 11

Fun Questions to Stimulate Discussions that can
    Go Deep and Strengthen Understanding! 21

Activities to Do… Together 35

The Appendix You Never Want to Remove!
    Quick Tips 123
        5 tips to handle in-laws and outlaws:
        family issues 125
        5 tips to keep money from mangling
        the relationship 127
        5 tips to stay in love despite
        different beliefs 129
        5 tips to build healthy relationships
        with your children 131
        5 tips to disagree with
        compassion and love 133
        BONUS: Our S.O.S. Formula 135

After-Party 137

Image Credits 141

About the Authors 143

Cuddle Up for Our Pre-Read Huddle

This is the book we have resisted writing! Here's our story:

When someone asks us how we met, we find great joy in saying we met playing Post Office! For the younger generation who may not understand, Post Office is a kissing game for teenagers that dates back to the late 19th century. This always draws surprised looks and lots of chuckles. Then we explain: We both worked for the U.S. Postal Service. In fact, Bil was on the hiring team that brought Cher into the fold!

From the time we began to realize we were destined to be more than coworkers, we have done things together! We worked together on various project teams; we are ballroom dance partners (and have won several awards as an amateur student couple); we have co-founded several businesses together, including a management consulting company, two publishing companies, and a non-profit events-driven spiritual community. And most importantly, we have built an incredible relationship together, based on communication, trust, understanding, and deep love for one another. We work together well … and people notice!

For years and years, our friends, colleagues, and even our clients have suggested—encouraged—even begged us to write a book about the secrets to creating a "perfect" relationship. The more people requested it, the more we resisted it! Our specialties include teambuilding, leadership, and spiritual enrichment—not relationship therapy!

Whenever someone asked us what the biggest secret was for a successful relationship, our answer always included three things:

- *Communication.* Deep, honest, intimate communication. The kind of communication where you share your needs, your issues, your dreams, and even your fears with each other.

- *Respect.* The kind of respect that would never say or do anything to make you partner look bad, and make jokes at the other's expense. Cherish the kind of respect that shows up as caring more about your partner's happiness than your own, and knowing your partner feels the same way.

- *Fun.* Sharing adventures, jokes, special moments of laughter together. Finding something every day to celebrate. Recognizing that in a relationship, fun is an attitude, not an event!

People think that our response is too simple—but here's the deal: While the words may be simple, they are not easy to accomplish! A successful relationship requires work and commitment, on the part of both partners. And it isn't always joyful. Sometimes you disagree—in fact, if you never disagree, someone isn't being honest in their communication! It's learning how to share different viewpoints, broach difficult subjects, handle rocky roads, and come out the other side stronger, with more partnering skills in your tool kit! And it is worth every moment, because as you grow together, it really is true: The best is ALWAYS yet to come!

So—why now? Why did we finally give in and create the book everyone seems to want us to write? Because we realize we have something very special—and we decided what we most wanted to share was not advice. You can go to a therapist or read a self-help book for that! We decided we would share activities! These are things we have done to help us grow into the incredible relationship we share. We've put in the time … and now we are ready to offer our version of a Relationship Playbook! We promise: if you put in the time together and do the work, you can build a relationship that gets better and takes you into a solid future together.

> *Maybe I don't know that much but I know this much is true. I was blessed because I was loved by you.*
> (Celine Dion)

There are regular relationships, and then there are 'significant other' relationships. If you find yourself fortunate enough to be in an intimate relationship with a significant other, you also understand how important it is to cultivate that relationship to keep it growing and thriving. When you make your relationship a top priority, you create the kind of 'significant other' relationship that is a 'spiritual partnership'—one that brings out the best in each one of you.

When you bond with your significant other, it's magical and life-changing for each of you. You enjoy one another's company. Just being around each other is nirvana. Your love life and intimacy are a top priority. Going 'all-in' with each other feels right. Neither of you has any inhibitions, insecurities, or reservations about deepening your bond with one another. Honest and open communication is valued by both of you.

Maintaining a sense of personal identity as an individual as well as a couple is valued and honored each and every day. Each of you prides your partnership as being able to find the balance between being a *me* and being a *we*. Each of you agree that a strong loving relationship is one that honors two strong, independent individuals who are committed to honoring their oneness as a couple.

This kind of relationship has many benefits. You:

- provide one another emotional support,
- are each other's sounding board on important life issues,
- are able to lean on one another during hard times,
- feel spiritually connected,
- have each other's backs no matter what,
- keep commitments,
- agree that open and honest communication and trust are key,
- allow each other personal space, and
- recognize that you'll always be there for one another.

A relationship this powerful and intimate doesn't just happen! As much as we appreciate the concept of "soul mates," we also recognize that this type of relationship takes work—on the part of both partners!

One of the critical elements of a thriving 'significant other' relationship involves spending time together, having fun, enhancing communication, and enriching each other's lives. In our work, we've heard the same thing over and over from couples who are struggling to create a deeper bond and connection together. While they recognize the need to spend time together, they end up asking the same question: What do we do together? You'd think the answer would be easy, but in this fast-paced, high tech world we live in, it's harder than ever to carve out the time and creativity to be together in relationship-enriching ways.

That's what this Playbook is all about!

❤ ❤ ❤

How to Use This Book

Do not read this book cover-to-cover! How many authors have ever said that to their readers? None! Until us! In fact, we recommend the best way to get the most out of this book is to be spontaneous with it!

This relationship guide is a sampling of the relationship building practices of couples who do things together, because they want to do things together! These relationship practices are some of the foundational practices that strengthen the incredible bond between significant other couples—bonds built of trust, communication, honesty, and vulnerability.

What's In This Book

There are four major categories in this book:

- ***Relationship Hors d'Oeuvres!*** That's our term for this collection of powerful tidbits of advice we've created. For each Hors d'Oeuvre, we invite you to spend time together "digesting" it. We've included a series of conversational prompts to stimulate your conversation. Remember, that is simply the beginning. Allow your discussion to dig deep and really have meaningful conversation surrounding each hors d'oeuvre you select.

- ***Fun Questions to Stimulate Discussions that can Go Deep and Strengthen Understanding***! We've discovered that one of the most relationship-enriching activities you can experience is deep-diving together into fun questions that allow you to authentically reveal your vulnerability with each other … risk-free! While these "Suppose …" questions may appear to be light-hearted and even somewhat shallow on the surface, trust us! Each one provides the opportunity for a deeper conversation that can be eye (and heart) opening!

- ***Playful Activities to Bring Fun to Your Relationship!*** One of the greatest discoveries we made as we strengthened our own relationship was the power of FUN! We also realized that we had to make fun a priority; otherwise, life just gets in the way! In this section, we are sharing a variety of activities that you can easily do together. It simply requires you to schedule the time and make it a priority! You're welcome!!

- ***An Appendix You Don't Want to Cut Out: Tip Sheets!*** We found that this book just would not stop writing itself! Every time we thought we were finished, we'd think of one more thing to include! That's why we added the Appendix, which includes a few Tip Sheets, offering our top five tips to deal with specific "pressure points" in relationships. We invite you to check out these tips, then add your own spin to the issues that affect your relationship. Plus (drumroll, please) we wrap everything up with our **#1 Bonus Tip** that can literally transform your relationship forever! (And it works in other situations in your life as well!)

Choosing What to Do!

Remember what we said: This is *not* a book where you work through the activities in numerical order. *We strongly encourage you to make the selection of an activity part of the entire experience!* Each activity stands on its own, and there is no particular order.

How do you make the selection part of the experience? We're glad you asked! There are lots of ways you can build spontaneity and fun into the selection of which activity you choose to partake! Here are a few examples:

- *Option 1:* Open, Point, Act! Just close your eyes, open the book randomly to a page, point, and go for it!
- *Option 2:* Random Drawing. Go through and number everything in the book! (Make this an activity in itself—where you choose colors and

styles to identify each item.) Then create a sheet of all the numbers, cut them out, and put all the numbers in a jar. When you're ready for some Relationship Play, simply draw a number out of the jar ... and that's the one you experience!

- *Option 3:* Allow one person to go through and choose a favorite activity for the experience, and introduce it to the other. (The next time, reverse roles!)
- *Option 4:* Choose what to do any way you want!

For the Playful Activities section, you'll find that each activity has a place to list the date(s) you use the activity, and a section for comments about the experience. This is useful as you revisit various activities and see how many different ways they can turn out!

Creating a journal to capture your experiences with *everything* you do in this Playbook is also useful. You can create a joint journal—or have individual journals which you can choose to share with each other ... or not! Just agree on the ground rules before you begin! And remember to date every journal entry! You'll love looking back over the years to relive your experiences and see how you've grown together as a couple!

We also recommend that together you tweak these activities with your own variations, so they resonate with your preferences and lifestyle—and then add new experiences that you create together! (We'd love to hear what activities you come up with!)

Final Thoughts Before You Begin!

One thing we've noticed with our own relationship, as well as the relationships of those we've mentored: the number one skill that brings a relationship together and keeps it growing is open, transparent communication! Your partner is not a mind reader, and it does not make sense to get all upset when someone does something you don't like, if you've never let them know it bothers you. Likewise, it is senseless to have an emotional upset because someone doesn't do something you really want if you haven't bothered to communicate your desire to them!

> *An example: We have a friend who came very close to getting a divorce because her significant other never remembered special days (like anniversary or birthday). Our recommendation was, if it is that important to her for her significant other to remember the special date, she should take the initiative to be sure it happens! Start mentioning it early by saying things like, "Our anniversary is coming up next week. What would you like to do to make it a special day for us?" or "Hmm... my birthday is Friday, and I would absolutely love it if you would ..." It literally saved their relationship!*

One other clarification about this book, who it is for, and how to use it: **This is not a book for couples in crisis!** If that's the case, we recommend finding a credible, well-recommended therapist. This book is for couples who want to deepen their relationship! The very word relationship, when used in the context of this book, describes two individuals who care deeply for one another and are creating a life together.

One of the best pieces of advice we can offer, in addition to transparent communication, is to do things together! When each person in the relationship grows on their own, it is no surprise that they typically grow apart instead of together. The activities shared in this *Relationship Playbook*, while seemingly simplistic, light, and easy, constitute a practice of building memories together, laughing together, sharing deeper information together, and enriching their life experiences together.

Enjoy these ONENESS BONDS, as together you create the nirvanic joy that'll define you both as the perfect couple, today, tomorrow, and every day in your future … together!

Relationship Hors d'Oeuvres: Thoughts to Ponder...Together

This section is one you will want to revisit often as a couple! It contains a variety of quotes, tips, and wisdom we offer, related to creating a strong, long-lasting, ever-growing life together. Whenever you turn to this section, spontaneously choose one of the entries and discuss it together. Be open and accepting of each other's responses, and practice compassionate communication and listening skills!

You can use these prompts and questions to get the conversation started:

- When I read this entry, I feel…
- The ways I agree with what this is saying are…
- The questions this raises for me are …
- What are some ways we can apply this entry to our relationship?
- What is this entry saying about us and our relationship?
- Digging deeper, let's talk about …

Relationship Health is really important! Here are seven love relationship 'vocabularies' that deepen our soulmate intimacy:

- sincere compliments,
- mutual encouragement,
- quality time together,
- just because gifts,
- sharing responsibilities,
- loving and respectful physical contact, and
- compatibility based on shared curiosity so you grow together and not apart.

Measure your relationship against these seven 'vocabularies' and identify what needs to be changed.

A genuinely fulfilling and lasting love relationship is available to all of us—if we raise our consciousness above the din of disbelief, above the feeling that it can't happen to us, above the doubt that we can ever experience such a love.

Base your relationship on unequivocal unconditional love, indisputable mutual respect and trust, loving memories, romantic moments, laughter and joy, playfulness, respecting your differences, making each other a priority, saying "I love you" every day, and many other soulmate intimacies.

Get a handle on your disappointments and anger. Uttering the wrong thing at the wrong time can steer your relationship in the wrong direction.

It's very important to remind your significant other how much you appreciate everything he/she does for you. Show your gratitude even for the smallest things. Don't take anything for granted, and let your other half know how special he/she is and that you treasure every single thing in your relationship.

No matter how open, transparent, and loving—your relationship can break down at some point. There'll be conflicts and hard feelings occasionally. You can cushion the hard landings of human infallibility by showing undying respect for one another and holding each other in high esteem. Otherwise, cracks will appear in the edifice of a once thriving and *wellthy* relationship.

Understand that each person in your relationship has a subjective experience of what you experience as a couple, family, friends, etc. Acknowledge the differing perceptions and impressions each of you may have. Work out any differences and biases as amicably, lovingly and respectfully as possible.

Consider your own beliefs and biases, so you can choose to modify, release or even replace the ones that may compromise your *authentegrity* and/or negatively affect your relationship. *(Authentegrity is our mash-up word combining authenticity and integrity!)*

Where your relationship is now may be the cumulative effect of your past relationships' mutual choices, habits, and shared outcomes—as well as your current relationships' mutual choices, habits and shared outcomes. Mindfully retool your relationship—as well as yourselves—to arrive at healthier relationship outcomes.

A lot of changes will take place when you're with someone for decades. And that'll mean loving each other through 'thick and thin' so your relationship continues to survive and thrive. And we're not talking about the 'small' stuff! Heavy stuff happens, things like: changes in religious beliefs and/or religions, becoming more spiritual than religious, serious life-changing injury, death of a family member (including children), end of life care for elderly family members, relocation, job loss, serious debilitating addiction, gender identification, sexual orientation, etc. The long term health of your relationship depends on your mutual adaptability, love and respect for one another.

Sow seeds of forgiveness and love. Release any and all grudges you are holding on to. Let them go. With forgiveness, you harvest the gold of a heart open to love, the gold of inner peace, the gold of a deepened relationship.

Avoid the following four unhealthy relationship behaviors that can literally destroy happy relationships and lead to the end of a relationship. We're serious. Avoid these 'four horsemen of the relationship apocalypse.' Rein them in immediately:

- Constantly criticizing your partner's looks, character and ideas ("You look like something the cat drug in." "You're so stupid." "That's another one of your moronic ideas."). Also, showing scornful contempt (putting down your partner privately and in public, purposefully embarrassing your partner and making him/her feel worthless and inferior)
- Cheating (infidelity)
- Habitually stonewalling (purposefully withdrawing from an argument or disagreement by filibustering any attempt to work things out)
- Blame-shifting (covering your own wrongdoing and intentional misconduct by placing the blame for your actions on your partner)

The phrase 'Patience is a virtue' is more than a cliche. It reminds us here are times when you must *go slow to go fast* —soooo, unhinge from adrenaline rushes that might cause you to plunge headlong into ruining your relationship, making simple mistakes, causing accidents, etc. Remind each other that infinite patience produces timely results in the long run!

Detox yourselves from toxic people—and you'll find inner peace. Declutter yourselves from unhealthy relationship clutter—and you'll enjoy inner peace. Retire from tiring circumstances—and you'll unearth inner peace. Vacate unfulfilling work as soon it's reasonable—and you'll achieve inner peace. Forgive each other for what needs to be forgiven—and you'll have inner peace. And when you both find inner peace, you enrich the love in your relationship.

If you're having less than perfect experiences in your finances, your relationship, your work, your health, your attitude, your life ~ recognize it's simply an outer manifestation of what's going on in your subconscious. You have the power to turn negative subconscious material into positive, life-affirming conscious thoughts, choices and actions concerning your finances.

Drop the 'r' and turn your *r*elationship with happiness into an *e*lationship with happiness.

Notice that when you find the right mix of open communication and respectful privacy, distance and closeness, your full disclosure and confidentiality exemplify how authentic your relationship will be.

Don't settle for a relationship that wants to sabotage your being true to yourself. Know your values, then build a relationship that honors and supports those values—and allows you to be the best YOU you can be.

Science shows that couples with an optimistic outlook tend to be more proactive when it comes to their health, have better cardiovascular health, a stronger immune system, generally earn a higher income, and tend to have a more successful relationship. So together, as a couple, strengthen your mutual Optimistic Spirit!

Forgiveness is a transformational tool for relationships, and adds to your health as well! A 2017 study by the Mayo Clinic found the following health benefits of forgiveness:

- Healthier relationship bonding.
- Improved mental and emotional health.
- Less anxiety, stress and hostility.
- Lower blood pressure.
- Fewer symptoms of depression.
- A stronger immune system.
- Improved heart health.
- Improved self-esteem.

Pay attention to how you are practicing forgiveness—which means releasing the grudges, and not saving them in some secret backpack to drag out at a later time. Forgiveness is a gift you give yourself, and it adds richness to your relationship when you are able to forgive and release!

Fun Questions to Stimulate Discussions that can Go Deep and Strengthen Understanding!

This section is designed to create a lot of fun conversations! Grab any one of the questions on the following pages, and enjoy a deep-dive discussion as you share your responses with each other. Get ready to laugh, explore, and grow closer together with these questions that stretch your imagination and get you out of the conventional boxes you may be inhabiting now! Have fun!

Suppose each of you were writing the story of your life, including the story of your relationship. What would each title be ... and what would the sales blurb say?

Suppose you could change you and your partner into various parts of a car. What part of a car would each of you represent … and why?

Suppose you could permanently change one thing about your appearance. What would it be and why?

Suppose you could bring back a famous person from the past. Who would you bring back, why, and what questions would you want to ask that person?

Suppose you could wake up tomorrow having gained an extraordinary extrasensory ability. What would you want it to be … and why?

Suppose you and your partner could be transported back to a particular period of history for a day (then return to the present), with the guarantee you would be safe. When and where would you want to be transported … and why?

Suppose you could take a pill that would destroy your greatest fear. What fear would you rid yourself of ... and why?

Suppose you could be the agent for any Hollywood movie star. Who would you select … and why?

Suppose you could live one day of your past in every detail. Which day would it be … and why?

Suppose you founded a non-profit organization. What would you call it and what would be its purpose?

Suppose you were an electronic gadget. What would you be … and why?

Suppose you could be on the filming set of your all-time favorite movie. What is the movie, and what would you like to do while you're there?

Suppose you and your partner could morph into a famous person. Who would each of you resemble … and why?

Suppose you could erase the worst movie or TV show ever produced? Which one would it be … and why?

Suppose you and your partner could spend a week with anyone presently alive. Who would you choose … and why?

Suppose you and your partner were granted one wish that you both had to agree on. What would it be … and why?

Suppose you never had to think about money, guaranteed you always have more than you'll ever need. What would you and your partner do?

Suppose you and your partner were circus performers. What act would each of you star in ... and why?

Suppose you could have one new skill, easily and effortlessly. What skill would you like to have, and how would you use it?

Suppose you could be reimbursed for the dumbest purchase you ever made. What is it you regret buying … and how would you celebrate your refund?

Suppose you were asked to describe the secret to a great relationship. What would you say … and why?

Suppose you could suddenly read your partner's mind. What would be the thoughts about you?

Suppose you had an honest urge for s simpler life. What would that mean for you?

Suppose you were given the ability to have any popular song named after you, because it represents something you believe in or represent. What song would you choose ... and why?

Suppose you could create a new tradition that you and your partner would celebrate. What would the tradition be … and how would you celebrate it?

Suppose you could be invisible for just one day? Where would you go, who would you see, what would you do?

Suppose you could change one thing about your childhood. What would it be … and why?

Suppose you were asked to identify the best thing about your current relationship. What would it be … and why?

Suppose you could trade places for one week with anyone in the world alive today. Who would you want to be … and why?

Suppose you were asked to identify the biggest red flag in relationships. What would you identify ... and why? And what advice would you offer to avoid that particular red flag?

Suppose you and your partner were awarded a one-hour carte blanche shopping spree in any store anywhere in the world (travel expenses included). Where would you shop … and what would you buy … and why?

Suppose you were asked to give an impromptu talk on the statement: "Wherever you go, there you are." What would you include in your talk … and how would you relate it to your relationship?

Suppose you and your partner were transformed into a holiday ornament. What ornament would you be … and why?

Suppose there is one thing you really want your partner to know about you. What is it … and why is it so important?

Activities to Do... Together

This section offers a variety of activities you can experience together as a couple! Each activity stands on its own, and there is no particular order. In fact, we recommend you choose an activity randomly!

You'll notice that each activity has space where you can add a date, along with some comments about your experience with the activity. It's fun to revisit activities, and compare results – and see how you've grown as a couple as well!

REMINDER: These are meant to be FUN! Don't overthink them, or create unrealistic expectations! Just be in the moment and enjoy experiencing each activity as it unfolds!

Food is symbolic of love
when words are inadequate.
(Alan D. Wolfelt)

Have dinner at your favorite restaurant ... and order something you've never ordered before.

Date(s):

Thoughts/Insights/Comments:

Love recognizes no barriers. It jumps hurdles, leaps fences, penetrates walls to arrive at its destination full of hope.
(Maya Angelou)

Take a trip to the beach or a lake. Take a walk barefoot on the beach or by a lake. Pay special attention to how the sand feels under your feet. Build a sand castle.

(No beach or lake near you? No problem! Collect some cardboard boxes and build them in the shape of a sandcastle. Cardboard egg cartons are cool to use too! If you're really creative, you can Modge-Podge sand onto your improvised castle – or you can just use markers to color it! Another option: you can make 'Moon Sand' by mixing together 2 cups of flour and ¼ cup of oil, then mold your castle together!)

Date(s):

Thoughts/Insights/Comments:

I never want to stop making
memories with you.
(Pierre Jeanty)

Think back on all your travels, and make a list of your favorite memories.

Date(s):

Thoughts/Insights/Comments:

I love you not only for what you are, but for what I am when I am with you. I love you not only for what you have made of yourself, but for what you are making of me. I love you for the part of me that you bring out.
(Elizabeth Barrett Browning)

Write each other love letters!

Date(s):

Thoughts/Insights/Comments:

We're all a little weird, and life's a little weird. And when we find someone whose weirdness is compatible with ours, we join up with them and fall in mutual weirdness and call it love.
(Robert Fulghum)

Share with each other your memories of the funniest things that have happened since you've been together.

Date(s):

Thoughts/Insights/Comments:

*Sharing food with another human being
is an intimate act that should
not be indulged in lightly.*
(M.F.K. Fisher)

Create a scavenger hunt meal!
Go to the grocery store and visit every food-related aisle. Pick one (and only one) item from each aisle. Then use your purchases to create your next meal together!

Date(s):

Thoughts/Insights/Comments:

True love stories never
have endings.
(Richard Bach)

Watch a funny movie!
It can be at a theater, on TV, streamed, or DVD. Your choice ... together!

Date(s):

Thoughts/Insights/Comments:

All you need is love. But a little chocolate
now and then doesn't hurt.
(Charles M. Shultz)

Buy (or make) a favorite dessert that you haven't had for a while.

Date(s):

Thoughts/Insights/Comments:

I believe that two people are connected at the heart, and it doesn't matter what you do, or who you are or where you live; there are no boundaries or barriers if two people are destined to be together.
(Julia Roberts)

Co-write a letter to a difficult situation you are facing as a couple, letting that situation know exactly how you feel about it ... and what outcome you desire.

Date(s):

Thoughts/Insights/Comments:

The best things in life are free. And it is important never to lose sight of that. So look around you. Wherever you see friendship, loyalty, laughter, and love ... there is your treasure.
(Neale Donald Walsch)

Take pictures of each other in fun poses!

Date(s):

Thoughts/Insights/Comments:

> To me there is nothing more sacred than love and laughter, and there is nothing more prayerful than playfulness.
> (Rajneesh)

Pudding paint a picture together!

Here's how: Mix up a couple of packages of instant pudding (different flavors for different colors). Lay out large pieces of wax paper, then create pictures using the pudding as if it were finger paint. (It's okay—in fact, it's mandatory—to lick your fingers!)

Date(s):

Thoughts/Insights/Comments:

Take my hand, take my whole life too. For I can't help falling in love with you.
(Elvis Presley)

Sing your favorite love song to each other.

Date(s):

Thoughts/Insights/Comments:

Make sure of this one thing: that the
person you choose to stay with is someone
you don't have to shrink yourself for,
cut yourself into smaller pieces for,
minimize yourself for. The person who's
meant for you will call you into higher
parts of yourself, encouraging you
to rise, to soar higher.
(C. JoyBell C.)

Co-write a resumè outlining your qualifications to be the perfect soulmate for one another.

Date(s):

Thoughts/Insights/Comments:

Love doesn't consist in just gazing at each other, but in looking outward together in the same direction.
(Antoine De Saint-Exupery)

Watch the sun rise in the morning.

Date(s):

Thoughts/Insights/Comments:

The regret of my life is that I have not said
'I love you' often enough.
(Yoko Ono)

Learn how to say "I love you" in different languages. Here's a start:

French: Je t'aime.
German: Ich liebe dich.
Italian: Ti amo.
Spanish: Te amo.
Dutch: Ik houd van u.

Date(s):

Thoughts/Insights/Comments:

We've got this gift of love, but love is like a precious plant. You can't just accept it and leave it in the cupboard or just think it's going to get on by itself. You've got to keep watering it. You've got to really look after it and nurture it.

(John Lennon)

Have an "out of season" holiday! Choose your favorite holiday, and celebrate it today.

Date(s):

Thoughts/Insights/Comments:

I believe there is a direct correlation
between love and laughter.
(Yakov Smirnoff)

Blow bubbles!
Yes, you read that correctly! Either purchase a bottle of bubbles or create your own, and have fun blowing magical bubbles together!

Date(s):

Thoughts/Insights/Comments:

I came here tonight because when you realize you want to spend the rest of your life with somebody, you want the rest of your life to start as soon as possible.
(When Harry Met Sally)

Share your memories about how the two of you met.

Date(s):

Thoughts/Insights/Comments:

In all the world, there is no heart for me
like yours. In all the world, there is
no love for you like mine.
(Maya Angelou)

Record the love letters you wrote to each other—each in your own voice. Play them for each other!

Date(s):

Thoughts/Insights/Comments:

I love people who make me laugh. I honestly think it's the thing I like most, to laugh. It cures a multitude of ills. It's probably the most important thing in a person.
(Audrey Hepburn)

Have a water gun battle!

Date(s):

Thoughts/Insights/Comments:

One cannot think well, love well, sleep well, if one has not dined well.
(Virginia Woolf)

Go to a restaurant neither of you have ever been to before!

Date(s):

Thoughts/Insights/Comments:

When I see your face, there's not a
thing that I would change,
'cause you're amazing –
just the way you are.
(Bruno Mars)

Be an instant American idol!

Make up a song together to the tune of "Row, Row, Row Your Boat" that talks about things you are thankful for; then perform it!

Date(s):

Thoughts/Insights/Comments:

It's fun to wander through,
The alphabet with you,
To tell you what you mean to me.
(Buddy Kaye and Fred Wise,
lyrics to 'A You're Adorable')

Play positive alphabet soup!
Come up with four positive words that start with each letter of the alphabet. Then create affirmations starting with "We are ..." and add the words! Here's a start:

A = awesome
B = bodacious
C = courageous
D = dynamic
E = enthusiastic

Date(s):

Thoughts/Insights/Comments:

One of the things that attracted me to Barack was his emotional honesty. Right off the bat he said what he felt. There are no games with him—he is who he appears to be. I feel fortunate as a woman to have a husband who loves me and shows me in every way.
(Michelle Obama)

Your daily word

Write each of the words you created from Alphabet Soup on a separate card or slip of paper. Put them in a container. Every day, pull one out and post it on the refrigerator or somewhere else that you see often during the day. This is your word for the day. Focus on it, and look for examples of it throughout the day.

Date(s):

Thoughts/Insights/Comments:

Love and magic have a great deal in
common. They enrich the soul,
delight the heart, and they
both take practice.
(Nora Roberts)

Learn a magic trick together!
Here's an easy one to start with:
Challenge your friends to tie a knot in a piece of rope without letting go of the ends. None of them will be able to do it, but you will!

REQUIREMENTS: A piece of rope or ribbon 3 or 4 feet long.

This isn't technically "magic," but it will baffle people who don't know how to do it. Hold the rope as in Figure 1 while challenging your friends to try to tie a knot in the rope without at any time letting go of either end. Then hand them the rope. When they give up, take back the rope and lay it down on a table.

Now for the secret move: Cross your arms before you pick up the rope! Pick it up one end at a time to make it easier to grasp. When you uncross your arms, a knot will appear in the middle of the rope, without you at any time releasing either end!

Date(s):

Thoughts/Insights/Comments:

The people who give you their food
give you their heart.
(Cesar Chavez)

Create napkin art together!

Use a cloth napkin to create interesting creations. Google "napkin art how to" for directions. Practice doing it, then invite someone over for a meal so you can show it off!

Date(s):

Thoughts/Insights/Comments:

Listening is love in action.
(Leo Buscaglia)

LISTEN!

Take a short walk together, and focus on listening. See how many different sounds you hear. After your walk, share what you heard with each other and compare your experiences.

Date(s):

Thoughts/Insights/Comments:

Don't take life too seriously.
Have fun in your life.
And, never forget my mantra –
love and laughter supersede all!
(Lisa Vanderpump)

Lie on your back and describe the cloud pictures you see.
As you each look up at the clouds, see how many different things you can see in them.

Date(s):

Thoughts/Insights/Comments:

Listen!
Do you want to know a secret?
Do you promise not to tell?
Whoa, oh, oh ... Closer!
Let me whisper in your ear,
Say the words you long to hear:
I'm in love with you.
(The Beatles)

Throw a coin in a fountain, river, pond, lake, well, or ocean.
Make a wish.
Tell each other what you wished for.

Date(s):

Thoughts/Insights/Comments:

Good relationships are based on kindness. On putting the person you love before yourself. On thinking of what you can do to make that person happy. Good relationships require kindness, commitment, and appreciation.
(Jane Green)

Give each other a foot massage!

Date(s):

Thoughts/Insights/Comments:

How do I love thee?
Let me count the ways.
I love thee to the depth and breadth and
height my soul can reach...
(Elizabeth Barrett Browning)

Let me count the ways...

Make a list of what you love about each other. Share your lists with each other.

Date(s):

Thoughts/Insights/Comments:

Nothing kills the ego like playfulness,
like laughter. When you start taking
life as fun, the ego has to die,
it cannot exist anymore.
(Osho, Indian Spiritual Guru)

A picture of our love!

Create a picture of everything you love about your partner. Then share your drawings with each other! (Don't worry if you can't draw! Use pictures from the web or magazines; use words and sketch art. Be creative and have fun!)

Date(s):

Thoughts/Insights/Comments:

Love is more than a noun;
it is a verb. It is more than a feeling;
it is caring, sharing, helping, sacrificing.
(William Arthur Ward)

Brush each other's hair, and give each other a great shampoo!

Date(s):

Thoughts/Insights/Comments:

At the height of laughter, the universe is
flung into a kaleidoscope of
new possibilities.
(Jean Houston)

Say each of the following tongue twisters ten times in a row.

Challenge each other to see who can say them faster!

A skunk sat on a stump and thunk the stump stunk, but the stump thunk the skunk stunk.

Unique New York.

A Tudor who tooted a flute tried to tutor two tooters to toot.
Said the two to their tutor,
"Is it harder to toot or to tutor two tooters to toot?"

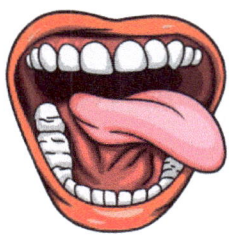

We surely shall see the sun shine soon.

Date(s):

Thoughts/Insights/Comments:

Never, ever underestimate the importance of having fun.
(Randy Pausch)

Create hand- and foot-print pictures in one or both of these ways:

1. Use finger paints
2. Draw around your feet and hands, then color them in.
3. Autograph your work!

Date(s):

Thoughts/Insights/Comments:

Loved you yesterday, love you still,
always have, always will.
(Elaine Davis)

Make a list of the highlights and accomplishments of each year (or month) you have been together.

Date(s):

Thoughts/Insights/Comments:

Love is when the happiness of another person is essential to your own.
(Robert A. Heinlein)

Tap into your inner artist!

Buy an inexpensive set of paints in the toy department of a discount store.
Create a picture together, by taking turns adding something to the work of art!

Date(s):

Thoughts/Insights/Comments:

If a person has made it into the inner sanctuary of the heart, where few enter, then I feel they are entitled to life membership, which means they will always be loved.
(Donna Goddard)

Separately, draw pictures to illustrate your favorite things to do together. Then compare your masterpieces! (Don't forget to autograph and date your work!)

Date(s):

Thoughts/Insights/Comments:

I saw that you were perfect, and so I loved you. Then I saw that you were not perfect and I loved you even more.
(Angelita Lim)

Replace something old with something new — then celebrate the release and the replacement!

Date(s):

Thoughts/Insights/Comments:

No matter where you go, I will be by your
side. Our unbreakable bonds mean
we will be as one forever and
face the world together.
(Aryan Arsh)

Do something you've never done before as a couple.

Date(s):

Thoughts/Insights/Comments:

A kiss is a lovely trick designed by
nature to stop speech when words
become superfluous.
(Ingrid Bergman)

Kiss each other — All Over!

Date(s):

Thoughts/Insights/Comments:

I'm scared of walking out of this room and never feeling the rest of my whole life the way I feel when I'm with you.
(from Dirty Dancing)

Pop some popcorn and watch an old movie.

Date(s):

Thoughts/Insights/Comments:

Finding someone you love and who loves you back is a wonderful, wonderful feeling. But finding a true soul mate is an even better feeling. A soul mate is someone who understands you like no other, loves you like no other, will be there for you forever, no matter what. They say that nothing lasts forever, but I am a firm believer in the fact that for some, love lives on even after we're gone.
(Cecelia Ahern)

Brainstorm your own list of other things you can do to add to this Playbook!

Date(s):

Thoughts/Insights/Comments:

> The beginning of love is to let those
> we love be perfectly themselves,
> and not to twist them to fit our
> own image. Otherwise, we love
> only the reflection of ourselves
> we find it them.
> *(Thomas Merton)*

THE APPENDIX YOU NEVER WANT TO REMOVE!!

What follows are Tip Sheets with some of our best ideas to handle specific issues that can sabotage a relationship before you know it! You'll find:

- 5 tips to handle in-laws and outlaws: family issues
- 5 tips to keep money from mangling the relationship
- 5 tips to build healthy relationships with your children
- 5 tips to stay in love despite different beliefs
- 5 tips to disagree with compassion

And a BONUS: Our S.O.S. Formula for Decision-Making (This one item can be a real relationship saver!)

Through my love for you, I want to express my love for the whole cosmos, the whole of humanity, and all beings. By living with you, I want to learn to love everyone and all species. If I succeed in loving you, I will be able to love everyone and all species on Earth. This is the real message of love.
(Thich Nhat Hanh)

5 Tips To Handle In-Laws And Outlaws: Family Issues

1. Openly talk about "pinch points" related to family, and come up with ways to work through them. (Example: We had one in-law who became unbearably frustrating with her small talk and negative comments about everyone and everything. When we visited, we had a mission to 'Keep On the Move!' As long as we were actively doing something, she was fine. So we stayed away from just sitting around talking! It was challenging and energy-draining—but also successful in keeping our sanity through the visit!)

2. Set your boundaries, communicate those boundaries clearly, and then honor those boundaries as if your life depended on it! (In fact, the life of your relationship just might depend on it!)

3. Give up trying to change someone! Those challenging folks we lovingly call family are who they are! Of course they can change—but it's their responsibility, not yours! So let go of the fantasies, and promise as a couple to support each other in the midst of dealing with the family issues. Give up the role of being General Manager of the Family Universe! Focus on acceptance of who they are, and choose NOT to be part of their drama.

4. Remember 'NO' is a full sentence! There are times when it is appropriate to choose to say 'NO' to requests from family members, or choose to separate the time you spend with each one rather than bring everyone together. The family scenes look great on TV—but in real life everyone brings their own script to family events! Make sure your script, as a couple, is clarified, understood, and well-rehearsed so you can create an award-winning experience!

5. Be fair without being fair game!

Marriage is a partnership, and couples
can't win with money unless
they budget as a team.
(Dave Ramsey)

5 Tips To Keep Money From Mangling The Relationship

1. Have an open, honest review of your financial situation, listing all bills, debts, and expenses. This is tough to do, but once it's done, you can be totally transparent in your conversations about your money.

2. Limit credit card charges! A great rule of thumb about money is: If we can't pay cash or fit it into our monthly budget, we probably don't really need it!

3. Practice the Principle of Recirculation and Release. In a nutshell, it says: Get rid of anything in your home that is no longer serving you! As you identify those items, choose together what to do in terms of recirculation and release: pass it on to someone you believe would really appreciate and use it; give it away to a thrift shop, Good Will, or other charity group that helps others; or chuck it in the trash if it is beyond use to anyone. (See our Circle of Release Activity if you have trouble letting go of things!)

4. Set clear, agreed-upon boundaries about money and how it is handled in the relationship. There is no one best way to do this. The key is to create those guidelines together, and stick to them. Items to include: bank accounts; amount limits related to spending without discussing versus spending only after discussion together; how and who holds what responsibilities related to bills; budgets.

5. Develop and practice a Consciousness of Giving and an Attitude of Gratitude, regardless of your financial situation. Have a conversation about what those two terms mean to you as a couple.

The best thing to hold onto
in life is each other.
(Audrey Hepburn)

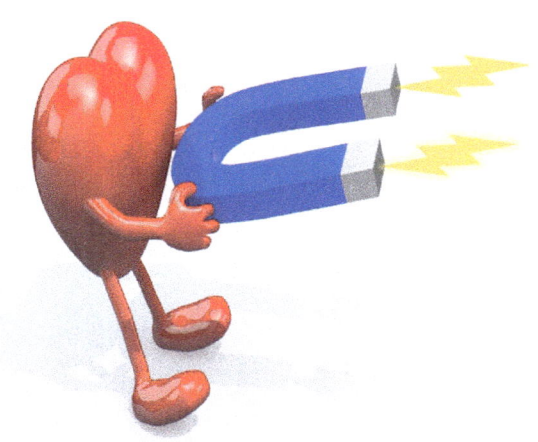

5 Tips to Stay in Love Despite Different Beliefs (Religious, Political, Values, Food Choices, etc.)

1. This one won't surprise you: openly communicate with each other to identify where your beliefs are dramatically different. Use a structured format for the discussion to avoid emotions interfering with the conversation. Here's one example:
   - Choose the belief you share different viewpoints about. This is the only belief you will be discussing. Set an agreed-upon timeframe for this discussion.
   - Each of you takes some time to identify three things related to that belief that are most important to them, and why.
   - Take turns sharing one item from your list at a time, with no discussion around it other than just sharing it.
   - Each person gets an opportunity to ask one question, then is silent while the other person responds. Then switch so the other partner get to ask, then listen.
   - At the end of the agreed-upon time, thank each other lovingly for their willingness to share what they believe.
2. Respect each other's right to have the belief they have. You may not agree with the belief, but you can honor the fact that they have it. It is not your job to "fix" your partner, or change their belief; instead, decide how you can live together in the midst of the differing beliefs.
3. Set clear ground rules around the different beliefs, and how you will talk with each other about them. If the beliefs affect the activities you participate in, lovingly clarify how decisions will be made.
4. Be willing to compromise when you can.
5. Be appreciative and express gratitude to each other for sacrifices, compromises, and honest communication!

Becoming a blended family means
mixing, mingling, scrambling, and
sometimes muddling our way through
delicate family issues, complicated
relationships, and individual
differences, hurts, and fears.
But through it all, we are learning
to love like a family.
(Tom Frydenger)

5 Tips to Build Healthy Relationships With Your Children

1. You are the ultimate role models for your children throughout their entire lives. No other person has a greater influence on their values and beliefs than you. So be sure you are good role models!

2. Make family fun nights, family outings, family vacations, family dinners, etc., center pieces in the way you do family! (You can even create your own book of Fun Family Activities—starting with some of the ones from this book that can be easily adapted for all ages!)

3. Agree together on the fine line between helping your children (no matter what age they are) and enabling them. Set clear boundaries together, communicate those boundaries, and most importantly, stick to them!

4. Communicate openly and honestly about your relationship, and how your children fit into it. Be open and receptive to answering questions, and remember that your children will move on into their own lives, while you and your partner are building your own "forever life" together.

5. Whether you provide your children with your genes or simply adopt them into your family, help them see that they've won the lottery for the most loving and nurturing home environment ever!

The greatest tragedy for any human being is going through their entire lives believing the only perspective that matters is their own.
(Doug Baldwin)

5 Tips to Disagree With Compassion and Love

1. Keep your discussion focused on the topic at hand. Don't allow it to escalate into name calling, bringing up old stuff from the past, or all the other things that bother you! Agree to be honest and clear with each other during your discussion. Remember, your partner is not a mind reader! Let your partner know what's on your mind, what you need from them, and why it is important to you.

2. Avoid blaming statements (you did this; you don't understand, etc.) and huge generalizations (always, never, etc.). Instead, learn to express your issues from your perspective (when you ..., I feel ...); be specific about describing an issue instead of broad generalizations.

3. This excellent tip comes from Brené Brown: When you feel hurt or upset by something you perceive your partner said or did, share with them by beginning with this phrase: "Here's the story I'm writing in my head right now."

4. Create an appropriate time and safe space for discussions where you disagree. Refuse to argue in public, when you are in a stressful situation, when you're hungry or tired, or when you find yourselves under pressure to complete a task.

5. Look for common ground. What about the topic can you agree on? Start from there. It may be as simple as agreeing that you love each other and want to reach an agreement!

With every experience, you alone are painting your own canvas, thought by thought, choice by choice.
(Oprah Winfrey)

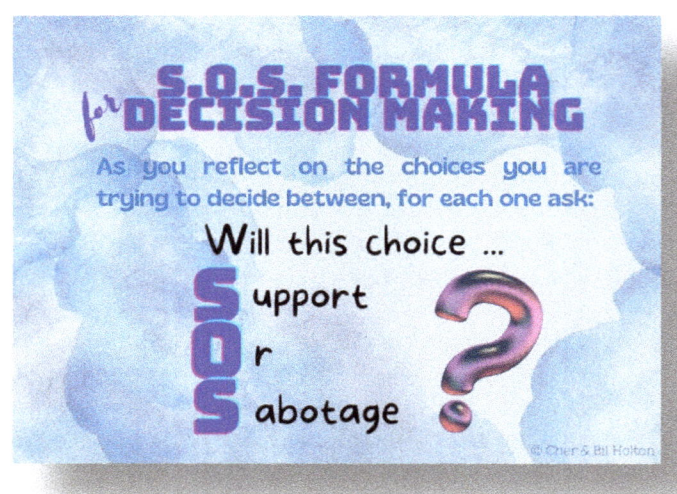

BONUS!!
Our S.O.S. Formula for Decision-Making

This is one of our favorite techniques for decision-making—and it works for so many different situations! We share it here for decisions related to your relationship; however, the same strategy works for decisions about habits you are working to break or build; eating choices; financial decisions; etc.

We call it the S.O.S. Formula. As you know, S.O.S. is an international code signal of extreme distress ... an urgent appeal for help. When you are in the midst of making a decision that has you polarized in your mind (or with each other), you may feel like sending out that S.O.S. broadcast for assistance! That's when this formula will be your lifesaving guide.

The formula is very simple—and very powerful.

S = Support?
O = Or
S = Sabotage?

Will this choice support or sabotage our relationship? Our goals? Our intentions? This one simple question can refocus your thinking, and bring you back to the priorities in your life! Remember, your choices create your experience—so choose wisely! Then, once you make a choice, move forward and do it with Authentegrity and joy!

In "normal" books, this is the section entitled "Epilogue" or "Afterword," but no one ever accused us of being normal! Because this book is meant to celebrate the joy of building strong, intimate, trusting, stable relationships, it only makes sense that our wrap-up should be a celebration of sorts! So we decided to call it the "After-Party!"

If you're reading this with us, that means you've made it through this book. Congratulations and huge kudos to you for everything you've done. While all these activities may *sound* easy, we can agree with you that they are neither easy nor simple! If you did them with any level of depth and intention, you discovered that these activities took you to places you've never been before as a couple. You've learned new discoveries about each other, elevated your ability to communicate honestly and authentically, added laughter and joy to your experiences, and created new ways to deepen the bonds between you.

We know these activities work, because we've used them all ourselves! People say we make it look easy to have a special love relationship, especially because we are able to live together, work together, and play together. We realize our kind of bond is not for everyone—and it is not our intention to create a cookie-cutter relationship mold for everyone who works through this book. In fact, our desire is the opposite! We want to help you create the type of relationship that works for you! We just want you to do it with intention and love.

Your next question just might be: Now what? We finished this book. So where do go from here? We have a couple of recommendations:

- Start over! Yes, you heard us correctly! Go back and play with this book some more. But as you experience the various activities again, be aware of the differences. Notice the new depth of your conversations; recognize how much more trusting you are of one another; appreciate how much you've grown as a couple since the last time you experienced each activity.

- Write your own book! Search for quotes that resonate with you, and have deep discussions about them similar to our Relationship Hors d'Oeuvres section. Come up with your own questions to ponder together. Create activities to try out together that stretch your limits and boost your fun quotient! *(An example: we decided to add what we called Indiana Jones Adventures to our life. Every month, we did one event that we'd never done before—something that stretched our limits and brought more fun into our lives. We each got to choose something. Bil chose white water rafting, fire walking, and sky diving. Cher chose ballroom dancing! By the way, the ballroom dancing turned into quite an avocation for us—we became a competitive amateur student couple and brought home several trophies! You never know where an adventure will lead!)*

When we began our journey together, we were 27 and 30, each of us with a divorce in our history. We knew we wanted a different experience as we built our life together—and we were willing to put in the effort to create our vision! Early in our marriage, we found a beautiful plaque with the following quote engraved into it:

Grow old along with me; the best is yet to be.

We loved the sentiment, and immediately posted it over our bed, agreeing that it was our relationship mantra. We were so young—and 'growing old' seemed like a lifetime away! Now we are in our seventies, and that plaque has traveled with us to every home we've lived in! Our journey has not been simple. We've certainly had our share of difficult decisions, heart-wrenching experiences, and even a few dark nights of the soul—but we've also had more than our share of laughter, enrichment, growth, travel, new experiences, and love!

No matter what, we always walked through these experiences together, knowing we had everything we needed within us to make things work! And we still hold that mantra in our hearts, and make it our wish to you as you build your relationship together: the best is truly yet to come!

Image Credits, used with permission:

Page 11	dreamstime_m_22777438
Page 12	207860914 © Skypixel	Dreamstime.com
Page 16	13135801 © Dirk Ercken	Dreamstime.com
Page 19	cherholton / graphicstock7ksSll_L
Page 21	134988386 © Elvira Shamilova	Dreamstime.com
Page 22	graphicstock and cherholton
Page 24	35977950 © Michalis Panagiotidis	Dreamstime.com
Page 26	dreamstime 1147334
Page 28	48886338 © Macrovector	Dreamstime.com
Page 30	1511861 © Dani92026	Dreamstime.com
Page 32	98638062 © Mohamed Osama	Dreamstime.com
Page 35	13238610 © Freeskyblue	Dreamstime.com
Page 37	clipart411947
Page 39	26242369 © Stockshoppe	Dreamstime.com
Page 41	47400471 © Multirealism	Dreamstime.com
Page 43	12573935 © Lxisabelle	Dreamstime.com
Page 45	66767439 © Drawinglounge	Dreamstime.com
Page 47	135129570 © Onyxprj	Dreamstime.com
Page 49	22439343 © Coliap	Dreamstime.com
Page 51	86030564 © Natis76	Dreamstime.com
Page 53	clipart-2755993
Page 55	173604751 © Inna Feshchyn	Dreamstime.com
Page 57	105188597 © Strekalova	Dreamstime.com
Page 59	16617131 © Tetiana Kovalenko	dreamstime.com
Page 61	49815114 © Iqoncept	Dreamstime.com
Page 63	15981271 © Sergey Galushko	Dreamstime.com
Page 65	202733753 © Dizain777	Dreamstime.com
Page 67	114806467 © Tetiana Zaiets	Dreamstime.com
Page 69	28690755 © Ermolaevamariya	Dreamstime.com
Page 71	30032527 © Shubhangi Kene	Dreamstime.com
Page 73	clipart 000682-0002-000354 and cherholton
Page 75	cherholton and canva.com
Page 77	45172654 © Cienpies Design	Dreamstime.com
Page 79	5330450 © Ldigital	Dreamstime.com
Page 81	11018061 © Connie Larsen	Dreamstime.com
Page 83	253429192 © Idalysshow	Dreamstime.com
Page 85	12351028 © Connie Larsen	Dreamstime.com

Page 87	27795299 © Photowitch | Dreamstime.com
Page 89	146814175 © Ernest Akayeu | Dreamstime.com
Page 91	8751685 / Cloud © Nadiya Struk | Dreamstime.com
Page 93	84054980 © Lena Meyer | Dreamstime.com
Page 95	132729599 © Colorscurves | Dreamstime.com
Page 97	129803456 © Pawel Talajkowski | Dreamstime.com
Page 99	cherholton and canva.com
Page 101	clipart.com and cherholton
Page 103	136414753 © Nitropen | Dreamstime.com
Page 105	20348150 and 119810505 | Dreamstime.com
Page 107	clipart and cherholton
Page 109	26417537 © Damedeeso | Dreamstime.com
Page 111	18250294 © Selvam Raghupathy | Dreamstime.com
Page 113	Canva.com
Page 115	140874950 © Yana Lesiuk | Dreamstime.com
Page 117	137569555 © Brridy | Dreamstime.com
Page 119	41042768 © Kamil Zablocki | Dreamstime.com
Page 121	28976756 © Mypokcik | Dreamstime.com
Page 123	91065486 © Almagami | Dreamstime.com
Page 124	94198324 © Kevin Lopez | Dreamstime.com
Page 126	47702024 © Christos Georghiou | Dreamstime.com
Page 128	46405305 © Fabio Berti | Dreamstime.com
Page 130	45955182 © Gzerosix | Dreamstime.com
Page 132	cherholton and canva.com
Page 134	cherholton and canva.com
Page 139	177362653 © Maria Brassett | Dreamstime.com

Cover Art Design: Cher Holton / Canva.com

About the Authors

 Bil and Cher Holton practice what they teach! They are marriage partners, business partners, ballroom dance partners, co-authors of many books, and overall "make life fun" partners! They know what it takes to make a relationship strong, trusting, authentic, and fun! They have a flair for the dramatic, a penchant for questioning unquestioned answers, an ability to think (and act) outside the box, and apply their deepest values and beliefs to their relationship.

In addition to a marriage that began in 1977, Bil and Cher have built a corporate leadership/team building business that began in 1983; a partner-publishing company that not only publishes their books, but also provides book design, ghost writing, partner-publishing, and coaching to other authors; a spiritual business that has grown into a non-profit events-driven ministry, creating a safe and enriching community for people who are more spiritual than religious. Through every business they build, they work together as a team to make it happen, while maintaining a thriving relationship in the process!

But it's not just work they do together! On a personal note, the Holtons like to push the envelope and maintain their zest for life by taking what they call "Indiana Jones Adventures," such as white-water rafting, sky diving, fire walking, experiential vacations, and ballroom dancing. (The ballroom dancing Indiana Jones experience became an avocation for them, and they've won trophies and awards competing as an amateur student couple! Although they've retired their competitive dance shoes, they continue to dance in the modest ballroom they've built upstairs in their home.)

Their dream is for every couple to experience the deep love, joy, and passion they have—and that's why they finally gave in to all the requests to write a book about relationships!

www.ingramcontent.com/pod-product-compliance
Lightning Source LLC
Chambersburg PA
CBHW041128110526
44592CB00020B/2728